A Garden in Hedon

Dan Hutcherson

ISBN-13: 978-0-9984452-4-3

Cover design by YeMi L. Hutcherson

This book is dedicated to the men and women whose sacrifice moved providence.

Table of Contents

Preface

It all started in 2012 on an overseas trip with my wife. I realized I was a Christian, though the full extent didn't sink in until many years later. I also returned home that summer with a phrase stuck in my head: "You cannot be given rights you already have." In hindsight, these events started a search for truth.

I was drawn to learn more about natural rights, the role of government, and basic economic principles. There was an insatiable desire to consume any book, podcast, or commentary that discussed liberty. All the while, I was evaluating my discoveries against the stories of my childhood, particularly the Fall of Man. I didn't know what I was looking for, but I found a personal God.

* * *

My journey resulted in an appreciation for the righteous traditions of Western civilization. I saw how God labored to restore the economic, political, and religious realms. No school of thought influenced me more than the Austrian school of economics. But any discipline of reason can only manifest through a moral population.

I began to notice the real conflict is spiritual, embedded in the nature of man. There is a battle for the human soul. The forces of good and evil became apparent, and I experienced conflict within myself. However, a silent voice guided me through the fog of war, and I came out as a living testimony to an eternal truth.

* * *

This book and its companion, *A Garden in Liberty*, are a product of my spiritual journey. I spent years texting little revelations to myself, then even more time distilling "my notes" into these books. I recognize the content to be groundbreaking but also mere reality around me. As such, credit must go where it's due.

I take full credit for the mistakes herein but defer all glory to God for any valid insight. He made the world with unimaginable depth and beauty. The influence of my late grandfather, Sun Moon, can also be seen throughout. His book, *Exposition of the Divine Principle*, provided the lens to unlock providential history.

* * *

This book contains twenty-one chapters, which are listed in alphabetical order. There is no intentional title arrangement other than placing the crosswalk first.

Each chapter was originally created as a two-slide presentation. The title slide provided a basic introduction, while the second slide wrapped content between its own introduction and conclusion. I have kept this structure intact throughout this book.

The section headings are what used to be bullets and sub-bullets within the presentation. They showcase a direct mapping between the family and nation. These parallels are maintained through the use of a vertical bar.

* * *

I wrote this skeletal book to carry out my personal responsibility. I desire only to record these self-evident truths, and I pray my observations require minimal correction by posterity.

Let your conscience be your guide.

Dan Hutcherson
Child of God

A Garden in Hedon

A Demonic Crosswalk

The Book of Genesis contains a demonic crosswalk.

* * *

The model of the Fall of Man extends into the fall of a nation.

God develops Creation | Invisible hand develops environment

The entire cosmos comes from God's act of production.
All natural laws, scientific laws, the standard for morality, and all relationships under the invisible hand stem from God (Genesis 1).

Lucifer seduces Eve | Government seduces consumer

The servant distorts God's Word through intentional lies.
The fears and insecurities of Eve, like the consumer, play out even though they actually hold the knowledge between good and evil (Genesis 2:9).

Eve seduces Adam | Consumer seduces producer

It's easy to blame Eve (Genesis 3:6) but it was Adam who was ultimately responsible, like it's the producer who decides what spirit to bring life to.
Adam and the producer must reject the impulse of immediate satisfaction with a compromised partner but we know that's not what happened.

Satan defines marriage | State defines market

Instead of waiting for God's invisible hand to determine the best time for marriage, the Fall of Man captures the market under an iron fist.

Cain v. Abel | Communist v. capitalist

The two fallen relationships (Genesis 3:6) give birth to two extrapolated societies locked in perpetual conflict.
Abel, like capitalism, gains God's favor (Genesis 4:4) even though he has original sin.

Cain murders Abel | Communist murders capitalist

Since the State embodies Cain's monopoly on violence through communism, it's only a matter of time that the promise of capitalism is murdered like Abel (Genesis 4:8).

* * *

The fight for freedom throughout history has been to rebirth (John 3:3) all relationships into one family and free market.

Apple of My Eye

The most powerful force in the universe is love.

* * *

Adam and Eve were naked and unashamed in the Garden (Genesis 2:25), and a beautiful marriage would've developed naturally within God's Word. But the temptation for fallen love was so appealing that Adam and Eve were willing to die to taste it (Genesis 2:17).

Love > Divine law | Wealth > Natural law

The allure of love is even stronger than divine laws (Genesis 3:6). This is like the allure for wealth can be stronger than natural laws.

Sexual relationship | Economic transaction

A sexual relationship, like an economic transaction, demonstrates the power of love.
It's a delicious apple, but there's a time and place for moral intercourse.
For instance, an apple is meant to be eaten ripe, like maturation is required prior to coming to market.

Lucifer sees budding love | Government sees emerging wealth

Lucifer lusts after this budding love, like governments lust after emerging wealth.
God didn't love Lucifer any less but the servant felt diminished in his own receipt of God's love.

Eve's temptation | Consumer's temptation

Eve, like a consumer, is easier to target as she's prone to more emotion and idle time.
Lucifer and the government appear wise and play into any existing fear or insecurity.

Eve and the consumer require patience while Adam and the producer develops.

Adam's temptation I Producer's temptation

Adam, like a producer, is harder to target directly as he's prone to less emotion and is out working (Genesis 2:15).
But Adam knew what sex was, like every producer dreams of reaping the reward of a satisfied client.
Adam lost his sacred honor by accepting love that was not yet his to receive (Genesis 3:6).

Children hide sexual relationship I Citizens hide economic transaction

Adam and Eve used fig leaves to cover up the place where the violation occurred (Genesis 3:7).
This is like citizens covering up the State's influence in economic transactions.
For instance, taxation is defended as a necessary evil or the price paid for a "civilized" society.
But this self-contradiction and immoral relationship leads to unnatural death.

* * *

The temptations of love and wealth have destroyed even the most powerful of civilizations. All it takes is one bad apple.

Barriers to Entry

The family has natural barriers based on divine law and parental forces. Adam and Eve were to wait to consummate their marriage with God's approval, like markets have a barrier to entry.

* * *

The Kingdom of Heaven is a self-regulating society since, as Adam and Eve demonstrated, the only alternative is death and destruction.

Barriers (natural) | Barriers (natural)

A family and free market has natural barriers to entry, both absolute and relative.

Divine law | Natural law

God warned Adam and Eve not to eat the fruit (Genesis 2:15), like it's a natural law to not violate natural rights.
These are moral absolutes that do not adjust to circumstantial changes.

Parental forces | Market forces

Parental forces have barriers to entry like house rules, cultural traditions, or national customs.
This is like a market having barriers such as economy of scale, high startup costs, or market regulations.
These are relative in nature and can adjust as the free market develops over time.

Barriers (distorted) | Barriers (distorted)

Satan and the State manipulate the natural barriers to entry, both absolute and relative.

Satanic law | Statist law

Satan lied about God's law (Genesis 3:1-5) and distorted a moral barrier to entry (Genesis 2:17).

Adam and Eve weren't ready for sex but they did it (Genesis 3:6) based on Satan's intervention.
This is like a market not being ready to transact but for State intervention.

Satanic forces I Statist forces

Satan's intervention with Adam and Eve (Genesis 3:1-5) distorted their relative time preference for sex.
This is like the State overrides natural market forces, regulations, and signals with its own preferences.

Garden of Eden (outside) I Kingdom of Heaven (outside)

Satan and the State's unnatural barriers create chaos and impose an extra burden on society (Genesis 3:14-17).
These violent regulations would not otherwise exist but for the State.
And the cost has been felt by every generation since the Fall of Man.

* * *

The only barriers to entry in the free market that will eventually exist will be those found under natural law and market forces.

Big Brother Bad

The violence of Cain and Abel comes after the sexual fall of Adam and Eve.

* * *

Humanity has never had a genuine, free market society. There's barely been a decent capitalist society ever since Abel was murdered.

Cain murders Abel | Communist murders capitalist

Cain and communists rely on their signature trait of immoral violence.

It's interesting to note that God didn't talk to Abel or stop his murder. He talked to Cain, warning that sin was couching at the door (Genesis 4:7).

Monopoly on violence | Monopoly on violence

Cain and the communists enact their violence directly or through the State.

It's a dog-eat-dog world where the competition is simply killed off, even if it has God's favor (Genesis 4:4).

Cain spawns living hell | Communist spawns communism

Cain and the communists create literal hell on earth since they are not their brother's keeper (Genesis 4:9).

Satan claims ownership | State claims ownership

Satan claims ownership via Cain and his sons (Genesis 4:17), like the State implicitly claims of ownership via taxation and regulations.

Providence of restoration I Providence of restoration

God's providence was passed to Seth (Genesis 4:25) and other Abel-like, younger sons.
But the default pattern of violence was already set by his older brothers.

Conflict among children I Conflict among citizens

The Fall of Man, punctuated by Abel's death (Genesis 4:8), ensured Satan's favorite children atop every level of society.

One family under Satan I One nation under State

Humanity will forever fight while it's the product of fallen love (Genesis 3:6).
It's only when a True Adam and True Eve appear can the conflict between children be resolved.
This is like only rebirth under market forces will transform inherent conflicts into brotherly love.

* * *

History isn't about shrinking the State or having some fancy constitution - it's about Satan's children being reborn (John 3:3).

Born From Above

The Tree of Life is blocked (Genesis 3:22) until you have been reborn (John 3:3). A True Adam is fundamentally different than anyone else because he is the original ancestor, the first to be born from above (John 3:3). He's like sperm ejaculated into Creation by God's breath of life (Genesis 2:7), and it is this central relationship that binds his family to God.

* * *

The fall of Adam (Genesis 3:6) was the lynchpin tragedy. Since God gave him the commandment (Genesis 2:16-17), he was expected to be the authoritative source on moral standards.

Cherubim (w/ flaming sword) | Servant (w/ weapons)

The cherubim protected the Tree of Life (Genesis 3:24) after deporting two non-citizens, Adam and Eve.
The servant of God is honoring God's Word at the border while another servant, Lucifer, turned into Satan by violating natural law.
This is like righteous governance is natural while the State is demonic.

Tree of Life (True Adam) | Tree of Life (Producer)

A True Adam brings life into Creation and whatever he touches.
He needs discretion on what to impregnate, whether its relationships or ideas.
This is like the producer brings life to something that previously didn't exist.

Tree of Knowledge of Good and Evil (True Eve) | Tree of Knowledge of Good and Evil (Consumer)

A True Eve cultivates life and has the discretion on who will be the father.
Eve could've waited for Adam on God's timing but brought death instead (Genesis 2:17).

This is like a consumer can patiently wait for a producer to develop or bring death by inviting the State.

Fruit of the poisonous tree | Fruit of the poisonous tree

The Fall of Man cut God out of the equation and made Satan the false father (John 8:44).
All the problems of the world trace back to a violation of first principles, starting with eating an illicit apple (Genesis 3:6).
Humanity itself is the fruit of a fallen, poisonous tree, hence the need for engrafting to the true olive tree (Romans 11:24).

Garden of Eden | Kingdom of Heaven

The children of God are connected by blood.

Naturalization (rebirth) | Naturalization (rebirth)

The only way to permanently cross the cherubim is rebirth via True Adam and True Eve (John 3:3).
This is a naturalization process where your past life must die to be reborn from above.
This is like a nation must give up its statist past to be recreated under market forces.
An unadulterated Garden would not have had a rebirth process; there would be no pattern of the Fall.

Citizenship (birth) | Citizenship (birth)

If you're born from True Adam and True Eve's family tree, citizenship is automatically passed hereditarily to every child of God.

* * *

A key step in returning to God's ideal is confronting who your parents are.

Devil in the Details

Original sin came from an illicit relationship with the servant. As such, there's a corrupted presupposition, pretext, presumption, context, or implicit bias behind how fallen societies operate.

* * *

Like the corruption of money, original sin is so nefarious because it's in our blood, passed down generation after generation. It taints every transaction.

Lucifer -> Satan | Government -> State

Lucifer was to honor divine law (Genesis 2:17), like governmental institutions are to honor natural law

They transform to become Satan and the State when they don't.

Purpose/intent | Purpose/intent

God's Word and laws were substituted but with malicious purpose and intent.

Lucifer was symbolized as a snake speaking half-truths via a split tongue (Genesis 3:1-5).

This is like the State using fraudulent lies to violate what it pretends to be honoring.

Monopoly on violence | Monopoly on violence

Satan and the State desire to be the final, monopolistic authority over human affairs.

But it's based on the perpetuation of aggression through fraud (Genesis 3:1-5) and the immoral use of force (Genesis 3:6).

Satan defines marriage | State defines market

Entering marriage and coming to market is presided by Satan and the State in the fallen world.

Eve conceives for Satan | Consumer conceives for State

Eve becomes bound to Satan, like how consumers are bound to the State.

These relationships birth children and downstream actors that are also in bondage.

It's no coincidence consumers, particularly single mothers, end up in bed with the State.

Adam seeds for Satan | Producer produces for State

Production always originates from an Adam or producer, even if they're fallen.

Adam spawned at least three sons (Genesis 4:1-2; Genesis 4:25) for Satan, like how the central bank produces for the State.

Because Adam turned away from God, this improperly but accurately makes Satan your father.

Christ alludes to the essence of this dynamic when he says "you are of your father the devil" (John 8:44).

One family under Satan | One nation under State

Since the marriage between Adam and Eve was claimed by Satan, all familial production ends up being claimed by the State.

The State becomes implicit owner over all life, love and property in the nation.

* * *

The cycle of immorality can only be broken by rebirth (John 3:3) into market relationships.

Draw the Line

The Garden of Eden didn't have borders until after the Fall of Man (Genesis 3:24). Since God cannot accept immoral lifestyles, even by His own children, Adam and Eve were expelled from the Garden. A servant guarded the border between God's and Satan's property.

* * *

We have to differentiate between the divided, fallen world outside and the united, pure world inside of the Garden of Eden.

Cherubim (w/ flaming sword) | Servant (w/ weapons)

A border agent blocks entry into the Garden of Eden in order to protect the Tree of Life (Genesis 3:24).
This is righteous governance with servant employees or institutions exercising delegated powers.

Garden of Eden (outside) | Kingdom of Heaven (outside)

This is a State-regulated society made possible only after the failure to self-regulate.
There are fallen children with differing degrees of immoral desires and self-destructive behaviors.

Satan claims ownership | State claims ownership

Satan ends up claiming humanity since the entire bloodline was tainted.
This is like the State manifesting its territorial monopoly on violence over the citizens.

Conflict among children | Conflict among citizens

History is a great illustration of the conflict within and between nations.

The power lust of the Cain-types exercise a greater degree of violence (Genesis 4:8).
This is like failing to be your brother's keeper if you support the State (Genesis 4:9).

Borders protect Abel | Borders protect capitalists

God wanted to work and bless the world through Abel (Genesis 4:4), so borders were created in order to help the Abel-types survive outside the Garden.
These militarized borders can be physical, legal, cultural, ideological, or sexual in nature.
They are unoriginal but necessary because of the Fall.

Garden of Eden | Kingdom of Heaven

This is a self-regulated environment made possible by the owners of true love.

God claims ownership | Invisible hand claims ownership

A True Adam and True Eve inherit God's love and property (Genesis 1:29-30).
They then reflect this love and property back to God to be used for His glory.
God can then proudly claim, "These are my children; this is my Creation."

Free association | Free association

The children are free to associate (or not) by trade within natural law.
This is like citizens interacting (or not) in ways they believe will be beneficial.

Lines of property | Lines of jurisdiction

The lines of love, including for personal property, exist between individuals within a family.
This can also be extended to the property lines between neighbors or the lines of jurisdiction.

* * *

As the Garden expands through the rebirth of God's children, the only borders remaining will be natural ones, but don't be murdered in the meantime.

Feel the Pain

There is always a cost, even if you don't see it.

* * *

Whether or not Eve was duped or caved to her own emotions, the fact it happened and the structure of the process is clear.

Eve violates divine law | Consumer violates natural law

Eve and the consumer are the first to be attacked and violate the laws of God.

Satan's intervention | State's intervention

The slow decay of moral integrity is synchronized with the equal advancement of immoral intervention.

Immediate gratification (seen) | Immediate gratification (seen)

The apple was delicious and pleasing to the eye (Genesis 3:6).
It appears harmless in the short-term but the long-term cost will eventually be seen or realized.

Satan enters marriage | State enters market

Instead of a matching and marriage under God's terms, it's Satan and the State that chooses the winners and losers.

Redistribution of love | Redistribution of wealth

Satan and the State distort what should be a natural distribution of love and wealth.
They leverage violent submission through the redistribution of love and wealth under false pretense.
This contrasts with God's righteous dominion through voluntary submission and intoxicating love.

Unintended consequences (unseen) I Unintended consequences (unseen)

It doesn't matter what the means of temptation is, but self-destruction awaits if you don't honor God's Word.

Eve and the consumer pay the real cost by experiencing the unseen, unintended consequences.

Painful pregnancy I Painful incubation

Eve and the consumer feel the weight of their decision (Genesis 3:16).

The experience of pregnancy and incubating a downstream need is a natural process.

But now there's the pain of taxation or regulations that otherwise would not exist.

* * *

Be careful with the little, seemingly insignificant decisions you make. They will always bear fruit, one way or another, as the consumer always pays.

Follow the Money

The Fall of Man passed down original sin through the corruption of Adam's seed. The production of God's seed went under Satan, like the production of money under the State.

* * *

The production of money is no different than any other product or service, except it impacts all future relationships.

Marriage signals I Market signals

There are a lot of natural signals within a true marriage or market.

Verbal/non-verbal cues I Direct/indirect prices

The tone or intonation in a conversation brings excitement or deference to an investment of love.
This is like market prices, both direct and indirect, influencing money being spent for the present or future.

Natural fluctuations I Natural fluctuations

There will be natural miscommunications, bouts of forgetfulness, or changes in preferences.
This is like the natural fluctuation in prices after a new trend is formed or a product goes out favor.
There's nothing inherently evil in this; it's just life and part of the evolution of love.
The key is that these relationships are not distorted by the State through, for instance, price controls.

Transfer of love I Transfer of wealth

A God-centered marriage expands into a family that overflows with love, which is naturally shared with others.
This is like a free market naturally accumulates and distributes wealth.

Marriage distortions | Market distortions

The State's distortions can be seen through the prism of God's Word and the natural laws around honest money.

Verbal/non-verbal cues | Direct/indirect prices

The same signals exist but they're distorted by Satan or the State.
The signals are now used to incentivize promiscuous affairs instead of marital relationships.
For instance, artificially low interest rates encourage a society of debt slaves versus savers who can invest into others.

Unnatural fluctuations | Unnatural fluctuations

Satan's moral hazard distorted Adam and Eve's moral compass and time preference (Genesis 3:1-5).
They chose to live for the present at the expense of their own and their children's future.

Misallocation of love | Misallocation of wealth

Entire family trees and industries are built upon the lies of fallen love and tainted wealth.
This is like the existence of zombie corporations that would not otherwise exist but for the State.

* * *

The return to health must include returning to True Adam's seed and honest money.

Free to Choose

All God wants is a partnership in love. True love must be given voluntarily under free will in order to even qualify as genuine love.

* * *

God sets the standard to not eat the fruit (Genesis 2:17). He may even warn you of the sin at your door step (Genesis 4:7). But God will always respect free will, even though He may not like the choice you make.

Adam I Producer

Adam and the producer are both masculine in nature.

Natural toil I Natural labor

Adam naturally works to plant his seed, like a producer labors to provide a product or service.

Painful toil I Painful labor

But after the Fall of Man, the ground was cursed and Adam's seeds were suffocated by thorns (Genesis 3:17-18).
This is like all the hard work by a producer is for not when the State ends up taking the harvest.
It creates a difficult, if not impossible, market for honest businesses to even survive.

Eve I Consumer

Eve and the consumer are both feminine in nature.

Natural pregnancy I Natural incubation

A woman's body was designed to conceive and birth children, which is bearing the natural costs of divine sex.
This is like the consumer naturally incubates and delivers downstream actors by bearing the cost of production.

Painful pregnancy | Painful incubation

But after the Fall of Man, the labor and delivery of children and actors became painful (Genesis 3:16).
Eve and the consumer always pay for the burden cost imposed by the State's taxation and regulations.

Garden of Eden (outside) | Kingdom of Heaven (outside)

The absolute respect for free will seems to have disastrous yet natural consequences.
Adam and Eve bore the fruit of their immoral choice (Genesis 3:16; Genesis 3:17-18), like a nation will reap what it sows (Galatians 6:7-8).

* * *

The lesson is, if you can't control your own sexual organ, then you can forget about controlling State power. It's not like you really have a choice.

Highway to Hell

The moral decay of society gives rise to the visible manifestation of Satan. After all, if you reject God, you replace Him with the State.

* * *

The Fall of Man was a two-part subversion of love.

Eve's fall | Consumer's fall

Eve's fall with Lucifer was spiritual, like the moral corruption of the consumer.

Eve appeases insecurities | Consumer appeases insecurities

Eve gave credence to her insecurities by entertaining Satan's lies (Genesis 3:1-5).

This is like consumers having similar fears and accepting State intervention.

Satan enters marriage | State enters market

Eve wasn't willing to trust in God's Word, and she allowed evil to enter into the Garden (Genesis 3:6).

This is like the State influencing consumers in order to gain a foothold in the free market.

Adam's fall | Producer's fall

Adam's physical fall with Eve was closer to God's intended vision, though it wasn't on God's terms (Genesis 3:6).

This is like a producer and consumer coming together but not under natural contracts.

Adam misallocates seed | Producer misallocates resources

Adam brought life to a coercive spirit, putting his sacred property into a tainted being.

This is like producers fall when investing resources into manipulated consumer demands.

Satan defines marriage | State defines market

The resulting marriage becomes abusive since natural laws are violated.
Satan and the State control both the marriage and market by violence.

Spiritual corruption -> Physical corruption | Moral corruption -> Material corruption

The spiritual fall led to the physical fall, like moral corruption will materialize financially.
It's an implicit spirit of coercion that eventually manifests into explicit violence (Genesis 3:6).

Servants of servant | Servants of servant

The children and citizens become enslaved by the servant.
This reduces them to servants of the servant, instead of children of God.

* * *

Breaking the pattern of the Fall of Man starts by honoring God's Word and not taking the bait.

It's About Time

Time is a valuable resource. As a natural constraint within God's Creation, it's only a matter of time before we pass away.

* * *

Since you can't serve two masters (Matthew 6:24), you'll have to choose whose timing to abide by.

Satan's timing | State's timing

The backdrop of Satan's timing is that it's self-centered and carried out with lies.

Time preference | Time preference

Adam and Eve came together in a sexual relationship (Genesis 3:6) that otherwise wouldn't have happened (yet).
The future production of children in a God-centered marriage was distorted into a present reality through lies.
This is like economic transactions are distorted towards immediate satisfaction through fiat currency.

Premature sex | Premature transaction

Adam and Eve were not ready for the production of children.
God specifically said not to eat the fruit (Genesis 2:17), so their marriage was cursed and brought death.
This is like the creation of lifeless markets and the death of honest markets.

Beauty bridled | Revenue bridled

Adam and Eve's natural beauty was suppressed, stolen, or otherwise transformed to satisfy illicit desires of Satan.
Their chosen reality led to a shortage of God's beauty in the world and an overabundance of living hell.
This is like price controls are used to satisfy the illicit desires of the State.

A shortage of goods occurs in the economy as revenues are stifled and underlying needs are not met.

God's timing | Invisible hand's timing

We may not always understand God's timing, but it always turns out to be the best.

Time preference | Time preference

The natural ebb and flow in time preference influences all production and consumption choices.
If you only invest for the future, you might go without in the present. But if you live only for the now, you do so at the cost of the future.

Premarital preparation | Premarket preparation

The season of life before marriage is a period of preparation.
Both Adam and Eve were to learn the skills required to be successful in the market.
For instance, God had Adam gardening and hunting before Eve even came along (Genesis 2:15).
Adam, like a producer in the research and development phase, was preparing to support his bride and family.

Beauty maximization | Revenue maximization

It's natural to fully express our God-given potential during each stage of life, especially given a finite window of opportunity.
A young child expresses a different form of beauty than an elderly person.
And there's no question young adults are at the height of physical vitality.
But as physical beauty fades with natural entropy, it transitions into deeper qualities like raising a new generation.
This is like a startup expresses a different revenue pattern than a developed market.
There's no question an early entrant in an exciting, new market can have high profit levels.

But as the market matures and profit margins tighten, it's beautiful to see downstream actors bloom.

* * *

It's about time we end the State's immoral intervention into our lives.

Leave the Beast

Secession is a necessary condition of a free society. Before the Fall, Adam needed to reject the unprincipled advances of Eve (Genesis 3:6), like an honest producer must reject consumer desires which are under influence of the State. But after the Fall, Adam and the producer need to "pull-out" because they're impregnating a problem. Context is key for this topic, and I'm focusing on the latter scenario.

* * *

Secession from God looks very different than secession from a servant. Only the Fall can separate you from God and your family, but secession from institutions should be just a natural function of the free market.

One family under Satan I One nation under State

The Fall of Man locked the family and nation in bondage spiritually and physically.

Servant identity I Institutional identity

Fallen people wrap their primary identity around a job, political party, or church.

Even their national identity is tied to the State or its political leaders.

Satanic law I Statist law

Satan and the State violates universal principles in their distortion of natural law.

Literal enslavement exists when coercion is used to prevent secession.

Providence of restoration | Providence of restoration

History is full of individuals taking responsibility and separating from evil.
Moses' "Let my people go" is an early biblical example, and the American Revolution is a more recent example.
These acts of civil disobedience could even be thought of as a holy divorce.

One family under God | One nation under invisible hand

Secession is the inherent ability to exercise additional responsibility over your own life.
Maybe they do make a political miscalculation but it's theirs to make.

Divine identity | Divine identity

Since identity is based on your parents, secession does not impact that relationship.
This is particularly easy through federalized governance where we are one nation under God.

Divine law | Natural law

There will be parental and market forces over the family and nation's free market.
But these forces protect and nurture in alignment with laws of God.

* * *

You should never accept fallen love like Adam did (Genesis 3:6). But you also can't force people to stay part of a paradigm they don't wish to be part of.

Lesser of Two

Biblical history shows God favoring the younger son (Genesis 4:4).

* * *

After Adam and Eve fell, God went straight to work salvaging what he could. The birth of Cain and Abel (Genesis 4:1-2) is parallel to the rise of two core economic systems, communism and capitalism.

Children inherit sin I Citizens inherit sin

Both Cain and Abel inherit original sin, so Satan could claim each by blood.

This is like citizens feel the State's monetary burden in both communism and capitalism.

Cain (older) I Communist (older)

Satan had a direct claim on Cain, like communism is the culmination of all statist ideologies found in history.

They both have a history of harvesting, enslaving, or outright eliminating their younger brethren (Genesis 4:8).

Satan/Eve (w/ Adam) I State/consumer (w/ producer)

Cain and communism are based on the Satan-Eve and State-consumer relationship.

Adam fathered both sons (Genesis 4:1-2), but Eve came to Adam under a fallen spirit.

Having sex with a tainted Eve was an immoral investment on Adam's part.

This is like a producer bringing life to further corruption by investing into a tainted consumer.

Rejected by God I Rejected by invisible hand

God did not work through or favor Cain (Genesis 4:5), like the communists have never been successful.

Abel (younger) | Capitalist (younger)

Abel still had original sin and the connection to Satan because of his parents.

This is like capitalism is more crony capitalism, crapitalism, or cronyism rather than pure capitalism.

Adam/Eve (w/ Satan) | Producer/consumer (w/ State)

God wanted Adam and Eve to eat the fruit but later on His terms, not Satan's.

The union of Adam with Eve (Genesis 3:6), like with the producer and consumer, is valid.

But it was premature and based on intervention by Satan and the State.

Accepted by God | Accepted by invisible hand

Since Satan claimed the first born, God resorted to working with the younger brother.

Abel was the controlled opposition that God could still show favor to (Genesis 4:4).

This is like development and progress of capitalistic nations are blessed if you compare their fruits to those of communism.

* * *

Abel is the lesser of two evils, but what God really wants is all children to be reborn into unadulterated, free market relationships (John 3:3).

Live Free or Die

Humans are blessed with the freedom and responsibility of choice. God's non-intervention in the Fall of Man (Genesis 3:6) illustrates that respecting free will is more important than coercing the moral choice.

* * *

God warned Adam and Eve that they would die if they ate the fruit (Genesis 2:15). Their mistake highlights that we can either live free or die.

Maturation to marriage | Maturation to market

Adam and Eve were destined to be together but on God's terms, like natural maturation to market without the State's influence.
The maturation of true love can only happen under free will, like honest wealth is only possible without the State's intervention.

Satan's intervention | State's intervention

God designed the fruit to be eaten ripe, but a temptation of fallen love happens before reaching maturity.
Fallen love, by definition, is a distortion of love that is inconsistent with God's Word and laws.
These falsities seem real, if accepted, but they always lead to self-destruction.

Garden of Eden (outside) | Kingdom of Heaven (outside)

God said Adam and Eve would die (Genesis 2:17) but they continued to live on, even having children after the Fall (Genesis 4:1-2; Genesis 4:25).
This indicates a life in sin isn't actually considered life at all.
The fallen life is the alternate reality that becomes the norm.
Since you can't be free and in sin, no nation will be free if individuals within it are trapped in bondage to sin.

Spiritual death | Moral death

Adam and Eve died spiritually, like a market in moral bankruptcy.
Adam and Eve, without their connection to God, were in the land of the living dead (Matthew 8:22).
This is like a zombie corporation that exists only because it's sustained by Satan.
The producer and consumer become centered on deviant interests that trace back to the State.

Physical death | Material death

Life on earth does have a natural expiration, so it doesn't have to be a demonic experience.
Our bodies naturally decay and return to dust (Genesis 3:19), like financial bankruptcy distributes resources back into the economy.
But the children and downstream actors have an unnatural bias towards death that impacts every area of life.
Death awaits as physical life and honest actors prematurely pass away.

Providence of restoration | Providence of restoration

When you realize how Adam and Eve brought death and destruction into this world, we have another choice to make.
We can choose to follow that still, small voice of divine intervention (1 Kings 19:12) to be reborn (John 3:3).
It's the choice to come back to life, though part of you has to die by letting go of the life we thought was real.

* * *

Choosing God is to live free and in reality. This is like a cell in the physical body of Christ coming alive for the first time.

Love Not War

War is the inevitable result of a culture of promiscuity.

* * *

It's important to be God-centered in all your relationships, not based on the State.

Satan seduces Adam/Eve I State seduces producer/consumer

Satan deceitfully redefines the definition of love (Genesis 3:1-5).
But true love and free trade exist in the absence of satanic intervention.
In fact, making love, like free trade, is inhibited if we accept this redefinition.

Bound with Satan I Bound with State

Adam and Eve's marriage, like markets under the State, are bound by the blood of abusive contracts.
Satan and the State can rightfully claim ownership over the fruits of these relationships.

Conflict among children I Conflict among citizens

Adam and Eve gave birth to children (Genesis 4:1-2; Genesis 4:25) with inherent conflicts at every level of society.
God didn't stop Cain from killing Abel (Genesis 4:8), so He won't necessarily stop State interventions.
But these conflicts and wars only exist as the direct result of free sex and a broken family.

Swords for plowshares I Borders into business

The marriage of citizens between hostile nations realigns human action to dissolve existing animosity.
The wasted energy that used to be directed towards war can be redirected into marital cultivation (Isaiah 2:4).

This is like free trade between hostile nations eventually breaks down the unnatural borders.
All participants have a vested interest in each other and moral incentives against war because they're too busy making out.

Garden of Eden | Kingdom of Heaven

The unadulterated Garden of Eden has pure relationships since Satan doesn't exist and Lucifer is aligned with God.
For instance, a divine marriage doesn't have Satan in it, like free trade isn't based on agreements made by politicians.

Interdependence | Interdependence

A network of interdependent relationships gets created where each participant contributes their divine talents.
The natural consequence of honest, open trade is both sides ensure continued success in all areas of life.

Marriage (family) | Market (free market)

A marriage expands into a family, like an honest market expands into a free market.

* * *

The model for peace exists at every level of society if you extrapolate absolute sexual ethics.

Made Me Do It

You can't blame the government for the failures of the people. It's Adam and Eve who consented to Satan (Genesis 3:6), like it's the people who consent to the State.

* * *

The deferment of responsibility is a major part the problem.

Divine law I Natural law

Adam and Eve chose to violate divine law (Genesis 3:6), like the people violate natural law.

Do not eat the fruit I Do not violate natural rights

The children of God, particularly Adam, knew God's commandment (Genesis 2:16-17) yet both of them fell (Genesis 3:6).
This is like the people invariably create the State even though it's known to be the biggest violator of human rights throughout history.

Consent to Satan I Consent to State

Satan could not be created but for the consent of both Adam and Eve, like the people must consent to create the State.
Their consent was manufactured (Genesis 3:1-5), not informed, but the fact remains that they knew better.

Satanic law I Statist law

Satan twists God's law by distorting language (Genesis 3:1-5), like the State manipulatively redefines words to serve its own interests.
The acceptance of this deviation from truth contains inherent contradictions that become Adam and Eve's chosen reality.

Deferred responsibility I Deferred responsibility

Adam and Eve both deferred responsibility (Genesis 3:11-13) when confronted about the Fall.

They first accused God then Satan in what is now an ingrained culture of blame-shifting.

Accusation toward God I Accusation toward invisible hand

Adam didn't just say Eve made him fall, he blamed God for it – "You put her here with me" (Genesis 3:12).
A producer falls into the same trap by blaming the consumer and the invisible hand.

Accusation toward Satan I Accusation toward State

Eve accuses Satan (Genesis 3:13), like the consumer blames the State.

* * *

Even though Satan lied, you can't blame the State for anything. Only you are responsible for the choices you make, especially when you know God's Word.

Means to End

Eve's insecurity towards marriage is like the consumer's insecurity towards the market. Both accept illicit intervention (Genesis 3:6) that destroys the future they desire and could've naturally grown into.

* * *

Eve wanted a certain end, to be like God (Genesis 3:5), without going through the natural growth and maturation process.

Lucifer seduces Eve | Government seduces consumer

Lucifer setup the first moral hazard in human history (Genesis 3:1-5).

Love > Divine law | Wealth > Natural law

There's nothing stronger than the allure of true love and honest wealth.

Even the temptations of distorted love (Genesis 3:1-5) are more powerful than any laws (Genesis 2:17), like the attraction towards the State for wealth triumphs over facts, logic, reason, and first principles.

Distortion of maturation | Distortion of maturation

Eve shortcuts the maturation process hoping to obtain the wisdom of love (Genesis 3:6).

This is like a consumer accepting the State's intervention hoping to gain wealth.

Eve fell prey to sin even though God gave her everything she ever could've needed to develop naturally.

She chose an unprincipled means in an attempt to receive an equivalent end (Genesis 3:5).

But her choice inherently violated universal principles and the equality of natural rights.

Eve's premature sex | Consumer's premature transaction

Eve and the consumer initially enjoy what they think is great sex (Genesis 3:6).
This is like there is some level of satisfaction via a State-coerced product or service.

Immediate gratification | Immediate gratification

Eve tasted the fruit (Genesis 3:6) and knew God's vision of good and evil (Genesis 3:5).
This is like the consumer's eyes are opened but the realization of being naked and ashamed comes after it's too late (Genesis 3:7).

Bound with Satan | Bound with State

The Fall of Man disconnected Eve from God and bound her to Satan.
This is like the consumer's relationship is consummated with the State.

Opportunity cost | Opportunity cost

Adam and Eve missed out on what God actually desired for them to have.
They gave up the chance of tasting the love of a ripe, fresh apple in marriage.
This is like producers and consumers give up a beautiful, robust market.

* * *

Even though the end appears pleasing to the eye (Genesis 3:6), the means must come through God's invisible hand.

Monopoly on Violence

Satan's moral hazard encouraged the destruction of humanity.

* * *

The protection of natural rights is one aspect of natural law. In it, there's a distinction between the moral use of force and immoral violence. For example, cutting someone in surgery versus stabbing someone in rage. This will focus on immoral interventions.

Escalation of violence I Escalation of violence

The first act of aggression (Genesis 3:1-5) came as a gaslight to Eve. It wasn't just an innocent misunderstanding of God's Word – there was malicious intent.

Lucifer seduces Eve (spiritual) I Government seduces consumer (fraud)

The first escalation is producing and reciprocating with a fraudulent lie (Genesis 3:1-5).
Satan and the State are great at quoting scripture and giving lip service to natural laws.

Eve seduces Adam (physical) I Consumer seduces producer (force)

The fraudulent lie inevitably escalates to the living lie.
The consummation and embodiment of the lie happened during the physical fall (Genesis 3:6).
This is like a fraudulent spirit turns violent once a producer brings life to fallen demands.

Satan supplants God I State supplants invisible hand

Satan creates a distortion of what God intends to create, though making himself the authoritative source.

The perpetuation of violence is the foundation for the State as it assumes a role outside of natural laws.

Double standard I Double standard

Satan's intervention inherently contained a perversion of natural law (Genesis 3:1-5).
This is like State intervention contains an implicit distortion of natural rights.
An unprincipled realm is created where double standards exist and universal principles are disregarded.

Immoral authority I Immoral authority

Satan and the State assume functions that can't be delegated by God and/or the people.
A true servant is limited to the delegated authority that it receives from its owner.
And the owner can only delegate what he himself has to give.

Spirit of coercion I Spirit of coercion

The lust for power in the name of love is never satisfied because it's trying to fill a God-shaped hole.
The spirit of aggression will unceasingly insert itself into every aspect of life.
It's not the actions per se, voluntary or involuntary; it's the coercive spirit behind the action.
Testing the spirit gets that much harder when its sincere people unwittingly acting on the State's behalf.
But they are of their father (John 8:44) and in need of rebirth.

Garden of Eden I Kingdom of Heaven

Just because force is used, doesn't make it violent – like changing a cranky baby's diaper.
And just because something is violent, doesn't make it immoral – like mixed martial arts.
That said, natural rights can still be violated without malicious intent.

For instance, accidents can still happen and immaturity will naturally exist.

* * *

The total elimination of the State is inevitable once all political violence is reborn into principled relationships. After all, a "limited Satan" is not part of God's plan.

Under the Influence

The Fall of Man brought humanity under the influence of demons.

* * *

The underlying influences reveal the reality of the situation.

Satan I State

Satan became jealous after he helped God with Creation but a new kind of love was given to children who didn't appear to have earned it.

This is like the State becomes envious of the growth, power, and productive energy of a budding market.

It doesn't seem fair that the producer gets the profit or the consumers gets the investment when the employees and civil servants were there first.

Lust for love I Lust for wealth

The central motivations for Satan and the State are jealousy, greed, envy, or another form of excessive desire.

This lust for significance knows no bounds as it preys on purity and innocence.

Perverse incentives I Perverse incentives

Satan and the State distract away from the moral choice (Genesis 3:1-5) by unnatural incentives that entice or discourage in ways that create a moral hazard.

Adam and Eve accepted this lie from Satan (Genesis 3:6), like citizens allow the State to influence market choices through subsidies and taxation.

Forced outcomes I Forced outcomes

Satan forced an outcome that went against God's will and what otherwise would be the natural outcome of the invisible hand.

This is like the State forcing love for seemingly noble goals but requiring the acceptance of immoral behavior as the means to the end.
All actions by Satan and the State lead to outcomes directly opposing God's intentions.

God I Invisible hand

God and a producer under the invisible hand are the owners who decide the purpose of their love and property.
They take the risk of investing love and should rightfully reap pure beauty in return.

Desire for love I Desire for wealth

God has the desire to experience love, like a producer desires wealth. But love and wealth is measured by active production, so they invest everything to be in a relationship with you.

Moral incentives I Moral incentives

God and the invisible hand have natural incentives that encourage the moral choice.
They can praise or punish in ways that influence human action, like markets can naturally subsidize or penalize activities.
For example, an immature producer, even a greedy one, is incentivized to serve the consumer before ever gaining profit.

Natural outcomes I Natural outcomes

The decisions made among the children of God in a free market will have natural consequences.
There will be a beautiful array of natural, spontaneous order in every aspect of society.

* * *

Accepting the devil's lies end up having the opposite intended effect since it's not under the influence of God.

Zero-Sum Government

It's not freedom when the State defines the rules of the game.

* * *

Lucifer saw God increase in attention towards Adam and Eve and felt a corresponding decrease in value, though nothing had changed in his own relationship to God. This lack of love mindset led to the creation of the State, where we all lose in the end.

One family under Satan | One nation under State

Satan owns all fallen relationships, so he manages his property as he sees fit.

Relationships (distorted) | Relationships (distorted)

Since Satan cannot produce, he must necessarily steal what God produced.
Satan stole God's children (Genesis 3:6), which led to Cain murdering Abel (Genesis 4:8).
These relationships end up becoming negative-sum because of the reduced productivity.
This is like economic transactions become abusive when coerced into taxation and regulations.

Standard of living | Standard of living

Abel getting God's favor (Genesis 4:4) doesn't mean Cain loses out in a zero-sum game.
God wanted to raise the standard of living for Cain through Abel, like even a communist's standard of living will rise if living in a capitalist society.

Cain murders Abel | Communist murders capitalist

Abel dies and Cain ends up spawning hell on earth (Genesis 4:17-24), like a communist will kill off every potential competitor.

We'll never know the beauty which capitalism can offer if savings are destroyed, investment is lost, and living standards are reduced for everyone, including Cain.

One family under God | One nation under invisible hand

A true family and free market expands in a positive-sum experience with increased productivity, labor, and love.

Relationships (natural) | Relationships (natural)

Human action revolves around relationships and contracts that aren't negatively influenced by Satan or the State.

Standard of living | Standard of living

The addition of a child or sibling expands the capacity to love, like the market increases in the amount of possible trade.
The creative pursuits by each individual generates a higher standard of living for everyone.

Mutual prosperity | Mutual prosperity

God's favor expands naturally to all of his children and servants.
This is like all actors in the free market are engaged in healthy, win-win relationships.

* * *

It's pure freedom when God defines the rules of the game.

Made in the USA
Monee, IL
04 November 2026

67377036R00036